World of Music

Western Asia

Kamini Khanduri

www.heinemann.co.uk/library
Visit our website to find out more information about **Heinemann Library** books.

To order:
 Phone 44 (0)1865 888066
 Send a fax to 44 (0)1865 314091
 Visit the Heinemann Bookshop at www.heinemann.co.uk/library to browse our catalogue and order online.

First published in Great Britain by Heinemann Library, Halley Court, Jordan Hill, Oxford OX2 8EJ, part of Harcourt Education. Heinemann is a registered trademark of Harcourt Education Ltd.

Editorial: Louise Galpine, Harriet Milles, and Rachel Howells
Design: Victoria Bevan and Philippa Baile
Illustrations: Jeff Edwards
Picture Research: Hannah Taylor and Fiona Orbell
Production: Julie Carter

Originated by Chroma Graphics (Overseas) Pte Ltd
Printed and bound in Hong Kong

ISBN 978 0 4311 1778 2
12 11 10 09 08
10 9 8 7 6 5 4 3 2 1

British Library Cataloguing in Publication Data
Khanduri, Kamini
Western Asia. - (World of music)
1. Music - Asia - Juvenile literature
1. Title 780.9'5
A full catalogue record for this book is available from the British Library.

Acknowledgements
The publishers would like to thank the following for permission to reproduce photographs: Alamy Images/ArkReligion.com p. 17; ArenaPAL pp. 7 (Orde Eliason), 26 (Jak Kilby); Corbis pp. 4 (Kalish/DiMaggio), 11 (John Van Hasselt), 13 (Reuters/Shamil Zhumatov), 20 (Royalty Free), 25 (Stephanie Sinclair), 28 (Frans Lanting), 29 (Kurt-Michael Westermann), 30 (Reuters/Sherwin Crasto), 34 (Reuters/B. Mathur), 36 (epa/Kerim Okten), 39 (Bettmann); Eye Ubiquitous/Hutchison p. 24; Getty Images pp. 12 (Yoray Liberman), 14 (Chip Somodevilla), 16 (AFP/Rabih Moghrabi), 23 (AFP/Indranil Mukherjee); Kate Vincent p. 6; Lebrecht/Paul Tomlins p. 18; Panos Pictures pp. 8, 33 (Jean-Leo Dugast); Photodisc p. 19; Redferns pp. 15 (Pankaj Shah), 21 (Ebet Roberts), 31 (Brigitte Engl), 37 (Tim Hall), 9 (Steve Gillett), 41 (Philip Ryalls); Rex Features p. 43 (Nils Jorgensen); Topfoto p. 22 (ArenaPAL/Jak Kilby); Werner Forman Archive/Private Collection p. 27.

Cover photograph of Indian man playing a *sarangi*, reproduced with permission of Corbis/Reuters/Jayanta Shaw.

The publishers would like to thank Patrick Allen for his assistance in the preparation of this book.

Contents

Some words will be printed in bold, **like this.** You can find out what they mean by looking in the glossary.

Welcome to western Asian music

The shimmering sound of Indian *sitar* strings; the wild, whirling dances of Turkish **dervishes**; the haunting song of an Uzbek woman plucking her **lute** – the music of western Asia is a fascinating mixture of different styles.

The Middle East

The Middle East is the area between Europe and Pakistan. It includes many countries including Jordan, Syria, Lebanon, Iran, Iraq, and Saudi Arabia. Over the years, there have been many wars in the Middle East and fighting still continues today. It can be difficult for people to play and listen to music in times of war.

Major cities, such as Beirut, in Lebanon, and Damascus, in Syria, are home to many people, but much of the Middle East is covered by hot, dry deserts. Traditionally, groups of **nomads**, such as the Bedouin, travel across the desert with their animals. Bedouin culture has influenced the music of the countryside where people perform songs and dances accompanied by a fiddle called a *rebab*.

This Bedouin man is playing a *rebab* in his tent. The *rebab* is played in many Middle Eastern countries and is the ancestor of the violin.

Central Asia

Central Asia covers wild, dramatic landscapes, from the rugged mountains of Kyrgyzstan and Tajikistan, to the sandy deserts of Uzbekistan and Turkmenistan, and the wide open grasslands of Kazakhstan. Many of these countries used to be part of the Soviet Union (a huge country that was ruled from the Russian capital, Moscow). In 1991, they became **independent** countries.

The Middle East

Middle Eastern people were playing musical instruments called harps and lyres more than 4,000 years ago. This is where the world's first cities began. Arabic is the main language of the Middle East. The word **Arab** is used to describe all people who speak Arabic, not just those living in Saudi Arabia.

This map shows central and western Asia, including the countries of the Middle East.

Map labels: RUSSIA, Astana, KAZAKHSTAN, 500 mi, 1,000 km, Black Sea, Caspian Sea, UZBEKISTAN, KYRGYZSTAN, Tashkent, CHINA, TURKEY, TURKMENISTAN, TAJIKISTAN, Kurdistan, SYRIA, LEBANON, Beirut, Damascus, IRAQ, IRAN, AFGHANISTAN, The Himalayas, NEPAL, Mediterranean Sea, JORDAN, ISRAEL, PAKISTAN, Delhi, KUWAIT, Persian Gulf, SAUDI ARABIA, QATAR, UNITED ARAB EMIRATES, OMAN, Red Sea, Arabian Sea, Mumbai, INDIA, BANGLADESH, YEMEN, INDIAN OCEAN, SRI LANKA

There are big cities in central Asia, such as Tashkent (in Uzbekistan) and Astana (in Kazakhstan), but most people live in the countryside and farm the land. Traditionally, many central Asian people were nomads.

While the central Asian countries were under the control of the Soviet Union, many traditional styles of music were forgotten. People were encouraged to listen to Russian music instead. Since independence, they have been trying to rediscover the old music and keep it alive. At school, children learn to play central Asian instruments, and musicians pass on their traditional skills of performing songs and poems.

Tengir-Too, a group from Kyrgyzstan, play traditional music. They take their name from the high mountain range between Kyrgyzstan and China.

The Silk Road

The ancient trading route from China to central Asia and Europe is called The Silk Road. The Chinese traded silk for all kinds of goods, including grapes, cotton, chestnuts, and pomegranates. The Silk Road stretched 6,400 kilometres (4,000 miles) across grasslands and deserts.

These musicians from Rajasthan in northern India are playing traditional instruments.

All about India

India is a vast country stretching from the Himalayan mountains in the north, across deserts and tropical jungles, to the beaches of Kerala in the south. Huge, bustling cities, such as Delhi and Mumbai, are crammed with people, but most Indians live on farms in the countryside. There are very rich people but many, many others live in poverty.

In Indian cities, audiences in concert halls are dazzled by brilliant musicians playing instruments such as the *sitar* and the **tabla**. All over the country, singing and dancing are a very important part of life, particularly at weddings, festivals, and other special occasions.

Types of music

There are many different types of music in Western Asia, from **jazz** to punk, and *bhangra* to *qawwali*. **Classical**, **folk**, and pop are three main types that are played and listened to in Asian countries. Music for voices is called vocal music. Other music is known as instrumental music. Music is often a part of other kinds of performance, such as film, theatre, and dance.

Classical music

Classical music usually follows strict rules. Most classical music was originally religious music, or music to entertain wealthy or important people. Classical musicians learn to play their instruments by studying with a teacher. At a performance of classical music, the audience sits quietly in a concert hall to watch and listen.

Folk dancing often takes place at festivals, like this Camel Festival in Rajasthan, northern India.

Folk music

Most Asian music is not written down as notes on a page. Instead, the performers make up the notes as they play. This is called **improvisation**. Folk music, also known as traditional music, is a good example of improvisation. The tunes and styles are often handed down over hundreds of years from one generation to the next. Folk musicians might learn to play their instruments from watching and copying family members. The music is played at special occasions, such as weddings and festivals, but it is also a major part of everyday life. Lots of people join in by singing, dancing, and clapping their hands. Folk music is often lively and exciting, with fewer rules than classical music.

Pop music

Pop music began in the 1950s in the United States and Europe. It is now popular in many Asian countries, too. Pop music tends to have a catchy tune and a strong **rhythm**, which is good to dance to. Pop musicians often use electric or electronic instruments. A lot of Asian pop music is influenced by western pop music.

This is the Turkmen group Ashkhabad. They are named after the capital city of Turkmenistan, and play a mixture of traditional and modern instruments.

Musical styles

All over western Asia, there are shared musical styles. Some styles of music, though, belong particularly to one area, or began there.

Indian classical music

Indian **classical** music is an ancient style of music and is closely linked with the religion of **Hinduism**. The music is made up of patterns of notes, called *ragas*, and **rhythms**, called *talas*.

In the north of India, classical musicians play the flute, the *tabla* drum, and lots of **stringed instruments**, which are played in different ways. The *sitar* and the *sarod* are plucked, the *sarangi* is played with a bow and the *santoor* is played with two hammers. In southern India, the most common instrument is a stringed instrument called a *veena*. A *veena* is like a *sitar* but has a softer, sweeter sound.

Other Indian styles

In villages all over India, music is a part of people's lives. This is particularly true during the many different festivals that take place over the year. Music in the countryside is often played in the open air. The styles vary from one region to another but singing, dancing, and playing drums and flutes are common everywhere.

Film music is incredibly popular all over India. People from all walks of life know the words to the songs from the latest **Bollywood** films. The actors and singers from the films have millions of fans.

Ravi Shankar taught his daughter, Anoushka, to play the *sitar*. They often perform together.

Ravi Shankar

Ravi Shankar was born in 1920. He is an Indian *sitar* player and composer. In the 1930s, when still a teenager, he performed with his family as a dancer and musician in Europe and the United States. He then returned to India and studied the *sitar*. By the 1950s, Shankar was well known in India and abroad. His two daughters, Anoushka Shankar and Norah Jones, are both musicians too. Ravi Shankar has helped to introduce the beauty of Indian music to the world and he is still hugely popular.

Middle Eastern music

In the Middle East, singing is the most popular way of making music, with instruments playing alongside the singer. Music is particularly important as a way of celebrating family events, such as weddings. In a city, people might watch a performance of classical music in a concert hall, go dancing in a club, or sit in a coffee house sipping tea or coffee and listening to a **lute** player.

Most of the countries in the Middle East are **Arab** countries. Their music is mainly influenced by Arab culture. The most common Arab instruments are the Arab lute, called the *oud*, and a fiddle called a *rebab*. There are also many **percussion instruments**, such as drums, tambourines, and cymbals.

This band are playing traditional
Turkish music in a coffee house
in Istanbul, Turkey.

Singing, dancing, and poetry

Poetry is very important in Arab music. In the past, Bedouin **nomads** had poetry competitions. They made up poems about heroes, wars, and the history of their people. The poems were not written down but the words of the winning ones were sewn with gold thread and hung up on banners. Today, Bedouin poetry, song, and dance still influence the culture of many countries in the Middle East.

In central Asia, singing and dancing are enjoyed by many people of different ages. There is a tradition of a woman singing alone while playing a stringed instrument. Many female singers can reach incredibly high notes. The words of a song often come from poetry. Long poems are recited or sung by travelling musicians at festivals and other social gatherings. Lutes and fiddles are played to accompany the singers and dancers.

Natural nomads

Central Asian nomads believe that plants, animals, mountains, water, wind, and other objects from the natural world have spirits. This belief is often the inspiration for their music. The Bedouin camel-drivers' song, called the *huda* song, is said to have a rhythm that copied the movements of the camels' feet.

A Kazakhstani hunter playing his *dombra* before a traditional hunting contest in a nearby village. Hunters from all over Kazakhstan gathered for the yearly competition.

The sound of music

The music of one area often sounds very different from that of another area. This is partly because different instruments are used. It is also because the notes are put together in different ways. A **scale** is a set of notes that goes up and down. Musicians from different parts of the world use different sorts of scales. They use different rhythms, too.

Asian sounds

Arab music is based on scales called ***maqaams***, which sound very different from European scales. There are *maqaams* to represent different emotions, such as pride, joy, love, or sadness. A musician takes a *maqaam* and **improvises** a tune around it.

Indian classical music is based on scales called *ragas*. A *raga* is a set of notes used as a starting-point for improvisation. The word *raga* is also used to mean a long and complicated piece of music that is improvised.

In Indian music, the difference, or interval, between two notes in a scale is often smaller than it is in a European scale. This makes the music sound different. Indian singers glide from one note to another so that there is hardly a gap between them. Indian musicians try to copy this gliding sound with their instruments.

The *tabla* is used a lot in Indian music. Its sound tells the listener that the music is Indian.

The *veena* is the main instrument used in southern Indian classical music.

Performing a raga

At the beginning of a performance of the *raga*, the musicians sit quietly and so does the audience. The *raga* starts with a slow, quiet section. Gradually, the notes and the mood are introduced. In the second section of the *raga*, the music speeds up. It becomes more lively and the tune is developed. It is an exciting moment when the *tabla* player starts to drum the pattern of the rhythm. Then the final section begins. By now, the music is racing along. The musicians' fingers are flying and the audience is totally absorbed in the performance, nodding their heads and tapping their fingers, until the *raga* comes to a dramatic end.

Moody ragas

There are hundreds of *ragas* to suit different times of the day and different seasons. Each type creates a different mood. For example, the *raga* called *bihag* is meant to be played and heard late at night, and has a mood of romance and longing. There is a story that a court musician from the 16th century sang a night-time *raga* at midday with such power that darkness fell on the place where he stood.

All kinds of instruments

The voice is very important in Asian music. There are songs about all times of life, from birth to death. There are happy songs, sad songs, funny songs, and many songs about love and marriage. Mothers sing lullabies to their babies. People who are working sing songs about their work. These might be fishing songs, harvest songs, or rice-planting songs.

Poems are often set to music. These are called **ghazals**. *Ghazals* are sung in the Urdu language, in India and Pakistan. They are usually about love and have a fixed number of verses and a repeated rhyme. *Ghazals* were first sung in Persia (Iran) about 1,000 years ago.

Fairuz gave this performance in Dubai, United Arab Emirates, in 2006. She was accompanied by a mixed Armenian and Lebanese orchestra.

Fairuz

Fairuz (born 1935) is a very popular Lebanese singer. Her name means turquoise in Arabic. She was born in the city of Beirut and started singing on the radio when she was a teenager. Later, she joined up with two brothers called Assi and Mansour Rahbani, who wrote many songs for her. The three of them worked together for 30 years and were very successful. Fairuz has sung **classical** songs, **folk** songs, and pop songs. Many of her songs are about love or about Lebanon. She has performed in concerts all over the world, from London to Las Vegas. Her voice has been described as sounding "like velvet".

Throat singing

In central Asia, there is an extraordinary style of singing called **throat singing** (*khoomei*). Singers move their mouths, tongues, and teeth in a particular way so that they can sing two notes at once. It is sometimes also called overtone singing. You hear a low droning hum at the same time as a high flute-like tune. This is a strange sound. Originally, throat singing was the way central Asian **nomads** imitated the sounds of animals, wind, and water.

These musicians are performing at a **Sikh** wedding. The musician on the right is playing *tabla* drums, while the other two are playing harmoniums.

Instruments with strings

There are many types of **stringed instruments**, from the **Arab** *oud* to modern electric guitars. Some instruments, such as the Indian *sitar*, are played by plucking the strings. Others, such as the Middle Eastern *rebab*, are played with a bow. The sound you hear is the vibration of the strings when they are plucked or bowed.

Most stringed instruments are made of wood. Different woods may be used for different parts of the instrument because one wood might be stronger than another, or might produce a better sound. For example, the body of an Iranian *tar* might be made out of mulberry wood, and the neck out of apricot or walnut wood. Strings were originally made of twisted animal intestines, then of silk, but now are mostly made of nylon or steel. These materials are stronger and cheaper.

Lute is the name given to a type of stringed instrument with a long neck and a pear-shaped body with a flat front. You play it by plucking the strings. The Indian *sitar* and *veena*, the central Asian *dombra* and *doutar*, the Iranian *tar*, and the Arab *oud* are all types of lute but they all sound different from each other.

Yair Dalal is a very famous composer, violinist, and *oud* player from Israel in the Middle East. He is shown here performing in England.

Shimmering sitars

To many people, the sound of a *sitar* immediately signals that the music is Indian. It is probably the best-known Indian instrument. The body of a *sitar* is made out of a decorated **gourd** and the neck is made of wood. There are usually 7 main strings and between 11 and 19 extra ones. These extra strings are called sympathetic strings and they vibrate when the main strings are played. Because it has so many strings, the *sitar* makes a beautiful, shimmering sound. *Sitar* players sit on the floor, usually with their legs crossed. The *sitar* is mostly accompanied by the *tabla*.

Sitars are often decorated with ivory patterns and carved wooden leaves. The tuning pegs along the neck are sometimes carved into the shape of lotus flowers.

Gourd instruments

A gourd is the hard, dried skin of a fruit or vegetable, such as a pumpkin, squash, marrow, or melon. The body of some instruments, such as the *sitar* and the *veena*, is made out of a gourd. Often, the gourd is beautifully decorated.

Percussion instruments

Percussion **instruments** make a sound when they are hit or shaken. Bells, sticks, cymbals, and gongs are all used in Asia but probably the most common percussion instruments are the many kinds of drums.

Drums come in all shapes and sizes. Most are made from a hollow container with a skin stretched tightly over the top. When the player hits the skin, it vibrates, and the air in the container vibrates too. This is the sound you hear. Some drums are hit with the hands and others are hit with sticks. Drums are played to provide **rhythm** for other instruments and to accompany dancers. They are also often played at weddings, festivals, and other ceremonies.

Indian dancers often wear bells around their ankles to produce different sounds. These might be loud, soft, or sharp, depending on the speed of the music.

Bartal echo

The *bartal* is a huge, heavy metal cymbal from northern India. It is so big that when it is hit, the deep, echoing sound can be heard for over 15 seconds.

Playing the tabla

The *tabla* is an Indian drum. It is used a lot in Indian music and its sound immediately marks the music as Indian. The *tabla* is really a pair of drums, one played with each hand. The smaller drum, called the *tabla*, is made of wood. The larger drum is made of metal and is called the *bayan*. Both drums have three layers of skin stretched over them, with a black circle in the middle.

The *tabla* is very difficult to play. The drummer makes different sounds by hitting different parts of the skin and by using a mixture of his fingers and the palm of his hand. The different sounds make different musical notes, so the *tabla* is not just providing a rhythm, it is playing a tune just like the other instruments. The *tabla* is usually played with instruments such as the *sitar* and the *sarod*.

Tabla players like Zakir Hussein use their palms and all their fingers to make different sounds.

Zakir Hussein

The *tabla* player Zakir Hussein was born in Mumbai, India, in 1951. He moved to the United States in 1970. He was taught to play by his father, Ustad Alla Rakha, who was himself a very famous *tabla* player. Zakir Hussein's energetic playing and brilliant technique have helped the *tabla* to become more of a solo instrument. Hussein has also accompanied many top musicians and dancers. He has worked with musicians from other countries and helped to spread the sound of the *tabla* all over the world.

Blowing instruments

Blowing instruments are called **wind instruments**. They are usually shaped like a pipe or tube. When you blow into the instrument, the air inside the pipe vibrates. This makes the sound you hear. Some wind instruments are played using a strip of cane called a reed. The reed fits into the mouthpiece of the instrument, so that the reed vibrates when you blow. The reed makes the instrument sound less breathy. Some instruments have more than one reed. Oboes and bagpipes are both instruments that use reeds.

A short pipe makes a higher sound than a long pipe. Most wind instruments have holes along them. You play different notes by covering different holes. Flutes, clarinets, oboes, horns, and bagpipes are all wind instruments played in Asia.

The ancient ney

The *ney* is a type of flute made of cane or reed. It is a very old instrument. *Neys* from more than 4,000 years ago were found in the ancient city of Ur in the Middle East, where Iraq is today. A *ney* has five or six finger-holes in front and one thumb-hole at the back. You hold it straight out in front to play it. *Neys* are still played in many Middle Eastern countries today.

In this photograph, Reza Derakshani is playing a *ney*.

The bamboo bansuri

The Indian flute is called the *bansuri*. It is made of bamboo. The piece of bamboo must be thin, straight, and about 75 centimetres (30 inches) long. The holes are burned into the bamboo because drilling would break it. It is vital that the length of the bamboo and the size of each hole are exactly right. If they are not, the *bansuri* will not sound right. String is then tied around the *bansuri*, partly for decoration and partly to stop it from cracking.

Hariprasad Chaurasia is a famous Indian *bansuri* player.

Bagpipes

The bagpipes are made up of pipes and a bag made of animal skin. They are played in many Asian countries including India and Afghanistan. Bagpipe-players blow air into the bag through one pipe. Then they squeeze the bag with their arm to push air out of another pipe. This makes the sound you hear. The bag stores air and allows the player to play a long note without running out of breath.

Sharing music

Sharing music is a very important part of everyday life all over the world. People sing together, dance together, and play instruments together.

Indian weddings

An Indian wedding is a very special occasion that lasts several days. Hundreds of guests are invited and the bride wears a beautiful red-and-gold **sari** and lots of jewellery.

At a traditional North Indian wedding, the musicians play a type of loud oboe called a *shehnai* and a drum called a *dhol*. The music is very lively and exciting, and really adds to the atmosphere of the event. There is also singing and dancing, with the guests joining in. There are songs to go with all parts of the ceremony, such as painting the bride's hands (called *mehndi*) and the moment when the bride says goodbye to her family.

These women in Gujurat, India, are celebrating a wedding by performing a traditional dance with sticks.

The end of life

In Kurdistan, in western Iran, a type of oboe called a *sorna* is played to announce that someone has died. Drums are played, too. Later, during the funeral, the dead person's family and friends gather around the grave. Songs are sung and musicians play the *sorna* and the tambourine. After a while, the musicians start playing faster, to cheer people up and take their minds off the sad occasion.

Dancing together

The *dabke* is a traditional dance in Lebanon and other parts of the Middle East. It is popular at weddings and other happy occasions. The dancers stand in a line, linked at shoulder level. The leader twirls a handkerchief or a string of beads in the air and all the dancers stamp in **rhythm**. *Dabke* means "stamping of the feet" in Arabic. Foot-stamping, together with jumping and kicking, are the main moves. The dancers also shout in time to the music.

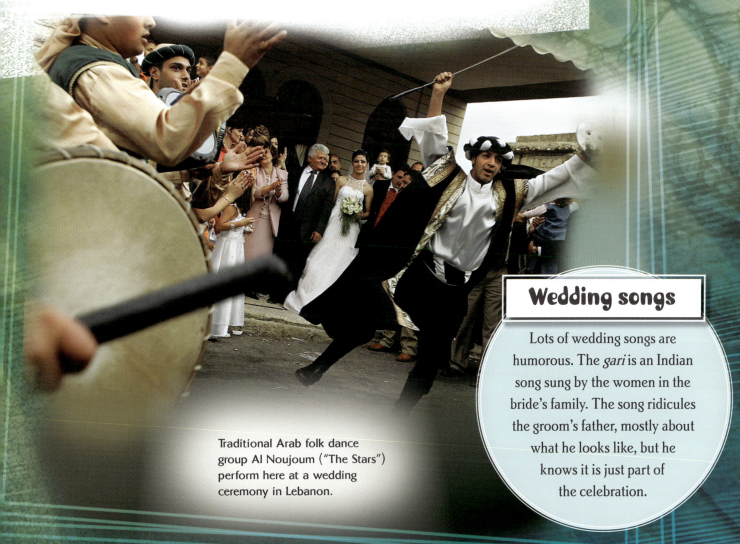

Traditional Arab folk dance group Al Noujoum ("The Stars") perform here at a wedding ceremony in Lebanon.

Wedding songs

Lots of wedding songs are humorous. The *gari* is an Indian song sung by the women in the bride's family. The song ridicules the groom's father, mostly about what he looks like, but he knows it is just part of the celebration.

Storytellers

A **bard** is a type of poet who recites poems from memory. In many central Asian countries, bards travel around the countryside, singing songs and reciting poems. They usually accompany themselves on a **stringed instrument**, such as a **lute** or a fiddle. Bards wave their hands around to add expression and there is often humour in their songs. They also recite in a rough, throaty voice that is quite different from a normal speaking or singing voice. This helps to create a magical atmosphere. It also separates everyday life from the world of the stories. Today, many bards also visit towns and cities.

Traditionally, most central Asian people were **nomads** who could not read or write. The bards visited groups of nomads and performed songs for them. The songs were a way of recording people's feelings, and describing what was wrong with their lives. Long poems often tell of the history of the local people and this is passed down by bards from one generation to the next. Poems that are passed on by word of mouth rather than being written down are called oral poems.

Rysbek Jumabaev is a bard from Kyrgyzstan. He moves his hands and face to bring his poems to life.

Shadow plays

In some parts of India, people put on plays using shadow-puppets. These plays tell stories from Hindu books. A light is shone onto a screen so that the puppets behind the screen make a shadow on it. The audience sits in front of the screen to watch the shadow-puppets moving around. During the play, musicians play instruments such as drums, cymbals, gongs, and flutes. There are singers, too. The sound of the music helps to create drama and makes the action more exciting, like the music in a film.

This Indian shadow-puppet is meant to be a princess. She is made of leather.

Hindu puppets

In some areas, puppets are only 15 centimetres (6 inches) high. In other areas, they are life-sized. There are puppets of people and of animals.

Temple festivals

During a temple festival, rows of mighty elephants parade along in a grand procession with musicians marching beside them. The elephants are decorated with gold-plated saddlecloths, bells, and necklaces. They also carry statues of gods and goddesses. The riders wave peacock feather fans to the rhythm of the music.

Thrissur Pooram is a good example of a temple festival. It is held in Kerala in South India, and has been a tradition there for over 200 years. Huge numbers of people come to watch and take part in the celebrations. There are spectacular firework displays that last well into the night. The entire festival lasts for 36 hours!

An important part of the *Thrissur Pooram* festival is the extraordinary musical performance called the *Panchavadyam*. Around 200 musicians take part, playing trumpets, cymbals, and different types of drums. They play their instruments incredibly fast and the music is frenzied and passionate.

This photograph shows a procession of musicians and elephants at the *Thrissur Pooram* festival in South India.

Holi celebrations

Holi is a Hindu festival in honour of the god Krishna. It is a noisy, riotous occasion where people wear their oldest clothes and then have great fun throwing paint or coloured water at each other. Everyone ends up covered in different coloured dyes. Processions of singers, dancers, and musicians join in the celebrations, marching along playing drums and flutes.

This snake charmer's *pungi* is made out of a **gourd**.

Snake charmers

Snake charmers visit towns and villages in India, performing at markets, festivals, and fairs. They sit on the ground in front of a basket and play a type of clarinet, called a *been* or *pungi*. The snake rises up out of the basket and sways from side to side, as if hypnotized by the music. The people watching throw money on the ground.

After a while, the snake charmer stops playing his instrument and the snake returns to the basket. It was not really hypnotized, just following the movement of the *pungi*. In fact, snakes cannot actually hear the same sounds as people. The snake charmer picks up the basket and the money, and moves on to perform somewhere else.

Bollywood films

Bollywood is the name given to the Indian film industry in Mumbai, the city where most Indian films are made. Around 1,000 films are made every year, over twice as many as in Hollywood.

Most Bollywood films are love stories or family dramas. They contain a lot of catchy songs, lively dancing, and bright, colourful costumes. The films are often funny, too. The dances are based on Indian **classical** or **folk** dances but many modern films also include western dance styles. The actors change their costumes frequently, sometimes even between the verses of a song.

Bollywood star Shilpa Shetty dances in a film called *Khamosh* (or *Quiet*), from 2004.

Bollywood films are incredibly popular all over India and other Asian countries. They are also popular in other countries where Indian people live, such as the United Kingdom and the United States. People of all ages and from all backgrounds enjoy watching the films and know the words to the songs. The films are a way of escaping from real life.

The actors in Bollywood films are huge stars, but most of them do not sing their own songs. Instead, they pretend to sing by miming to the words, often while they are dancing. The singer whose voice you hear does not actually appear in the film. Despite this, many film singers who are never seen on screen are as popular as the actors. Some have been doing the job for many years. A film with good songs is more likely to be successful.

Asha Bhosle has been singing film songs behind the scenes for 60 years.

Asha Bhosle

Asha Bhosle is one of the most famous film singers in India. She was born into a family of musicians in 1933. As a child, she moved to Mumbai. She sang her first film song when she was only 10 years old. Since then, she has sung on hundreds of films. One of her biggest films, released in 1995, was called *Rangeela*. Asha is now a grandmother, but she can still sound like a young girl when she sings.

Music and religion

The main Asian religions are **Hinduism** and **Islam**. About 90 per cent of Indian people are Hindus. Most people in the Middle East and central Asia are Muslims and follow Islam.

Music and Hinduism

Hinduism is one of the world's oldest religions. Hindus believe that after death, a person's soul is born again into another body. This is called reincarnation. They also believe in many gods and goddesses, including Vishnu, Shiva, and Lakshmi. All the gods have different personalities and Hindus pray to them for different reasons.

Indian music is closely linked to Hinduism. For many Hindus, playing and listening to music is a deeply spiritual experience. It is a way of getting closer to the gods. Indian classical music developed from the religious music performed in temples and **shrines** all over the country. Hindus today use music as a way of sharing their religion. Music is particularly important in temples on festival days when Hindu worshippers thank their gods and honour them with prayers and songs.

Hindu songs

A *bhajan* is a Hindu sacred song in praise of gods or goddesses. A group of people sing together, with one of them as leader. They often close their eyes to help them to concentrate. *Bhajans* can be very old songs, with simple tunes and lots of repeated words. The themes of the songs are descriptions of the gods and stories from their lives. *Bhajan* singers are usually accompanied by **classical** music played on instruments such as the *veena*, the *sarangi*, the flute, or the *tabla*.

Krishna's flute

Hindus worship the god Krishna as a great hero. His adventures are described in the book called the *Mahabharata*. There are many stories about Krishna playing his flute to the young milkmaids. He plays so beautifully that the maidens fall in love with him and their lost cattle come back to him. Krishna holds his flute to the side, like a modern player in an orchestra, rather than straight out in front.

Indian dancing

Indian people from all walks of life enjoy dancing at weddings, parties, festivals, or other special occasions. Indian classical dance, though, is a serious form of art based on Hindu beliefs. The dances usually have a religious theme. Traditionally, they were performed in temples but now people go to watch them in theatres too.

Dancers train hard for many years. In performances, they are accompanied by singers and by traditional instruments. Dancers and musicians work closely together and attention to detail is very important. There are different styles of classical dance including *Kathak*, *Kathakali*, *Manipuri*, and *Odissi*.

These Indian dancers are performing the classical style of dance called *Odissi*.

Hands and faces

Dancers have incredible control over the muscles in their faces. This means they can move each eyebrow on its own, each cheek on its own, and so on. They also move their eyes in exaggerated ways. They use facial expressions to show different emotions. For example, there are nine main facial expressions in *Kathakali* dancing: love, humour, fear, sadness, anger, courage, disgust, wonder, and peace.

Indian dancers use all kinds of hand actions during a performance. These actions are called *mudras* and they help the dancer to tell the story. Each action means something different. For example, holding one hand in a particular way means "eagle". Holding it in a different way means "moon".

Split personalities

Some dancers have such control over their face muscles that they can laugh with one side of their face and cry with the other at the same time.

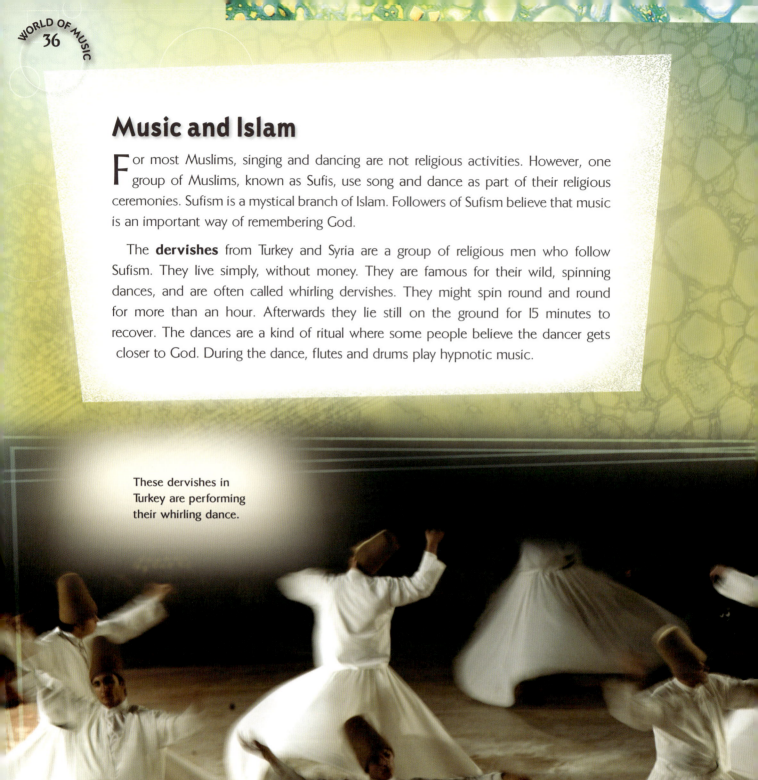

Music and Islam

For most Muslims, singing and dancing are not religious activities. However, one group of Muslims, known as Sufis, use song and dance as part of their religious ceremonies. Sufism is a mystical branch of Islam. Followers of Sufism believe that music is an important way of remembering God.

The **dervishes** from Turkey and Syria are a group of religious men who follow Sufism. They live simply, without money. They are famous for their wild, spinning dances, and are often called whirling dervishes. They might spin round and round for more than an hour. Afterwards they lie still on the ground for 15 minutes to recover. The dances are a kind of ritual where some people believe the dancer gets closer to God. During the dance, flutes and drums play hypnotic music.

These dervishes in Turkey are performing their whirling dance.

Qawwali is a kind of Sufi music from Pakistan and north India. The music first appeared in the 1200s and was traditionally sung at the shrines of Sufi saints. *Qawwali* music has a pulsating beat, a dramatic singing style, and a message of love and peace. The musicians are trying to create a link to God, both for themselves and for their audience.

Qawwali music is performed by a group of men called a party. There is a lead singer, one or two other singers who play an instrument called a harmonium, at least one percussion-player, and a chorus of singers who clap in **rhythm**. The words of the songs often come from poems about love. Sufis believe this is the love between themselves and God, rather than the love between two people. The tradition of *qawwali* singing is passed down within families.

Nusrat Fateh Ali Khan was a very famous *qawwali* singer.

Nusrat Fateh Ali Khan

The best-known *qawwali* musician was the Pakistani singer Nusrat Fateh Ali Khan. Born in 1948, he performed at many concerts and made records in Pakistan, Europe, and the United States. His main ambition was to spread a message of peace and love. Khan had an amazing voice and was loved by millions of fans all over the world. He died in 1997.

A changing world

During the latter part of the 20th century, many new technologies were introduced to the world of music. These included electronic instruments, such as synthesizers and drum machines, and computerized ways of recording music. All this has changed the way some music is played and listened to.

Influencing each other

As communication and travel become easier, musicians from different cultures borrow from each other's music. Western **classical** music has been enjoyed in Asian countries for many years. Now many western pop musicians are also popular in Asia and are influencing the musicians there. Elton John, for example, is a popular performer in India and the Middle East. Western musicians are also influenced by **folk** or classical music from Asia. Many western pop musicians use Asian instruments, such as the *tabla*, to create different sounds.

Bollywood films have also been influenced by western culture. The songs often have a western pop sound. The plots are becoming less traditional too. For example, young people are now more likely to be shown meeting at a disco rather than at their parents' houses.

Forbidden kisses

In modern Bollywood films, the actors are allowed to kiss each other on screen. This never happened in traditional Bollywood films!

Ravi Shankar and The Beatles

In the mid-1960s, the British pop group The Beatles became interested in Indian music. They travelled to India, met Indian musicians, and discovered Indian musical instruments. The influence of Indian music can be heard in some of their songs. For example, on the song "Norwegian Wood", they used a *sitar*. The Beatles were one of the first pop groups to try out Asian instruments. At that time, most pop musicians only used guitars and drums.

The musician who influenced The Beatles most of all was Ravi Shankar. He taught one of the group, George Harrison, to play the *sitar*. Later, the two of them performed together in concerts.

In this picture from 1967, Beatle George Harrison listens as Ravi Shankar plays his *sitar*.

Global music

The word "globalization" describes the way in which the same things happen or are available all over the world. In music, it could mean that you can go to a music shop in New York and buy a CD of Lebanese folk music. Or that in an Indian city such as Delhi, you can go to a western pop music concert.

Globalization has happened because new technology has made it easier for people who do not live near each other to communicate with each other. Travelling from one country to another is also much easier and cheaper than it used to be. Cable and satellite television have introduced pop music from Europe and the United States to other parts of the world, including Asia.

Globalization can be a good thing. For example, it introduces people to styles of music they might not otherwise hear. Sometimes, though, it can mean that people stop listening to local or traditional styles, which then disappear. It can also mean that music becomes the same all over the world.

Mixing the old and the new

Asian pop music is often a mixture, or **fusion**, of traditional and modern styles. A band called The Urker from Kazakhstan makes pop videos that are influenced by western pop videos in their style and design. But the videos are filmed in Kazakhstan and often contain traditional costumes and scenery typical of the area. The band plays a mixture of traditional instruments, such as a type of **lute** called a *dombra* and a fiddle called a *kobyz*, and modern pop instruments, such as electric guitars and drums. Their songs are inspired both by the folk music of Kazakhstan and by western pop songs.

Here is Sevara Nazarkhan, singing and playing her *doutar*.

Sevara Nazarkhan

Sevara Nazarkhan (above) was born in 1978, and is a singer, songwriter, and musician from Uzbekistan in central Asia. She plays a kind of lute called a *doutar*. Her instrument is traditional and she is clearly inspired by local music. But she is also influenced by western pop styles. In Uzbekistan, she is seen as a pop star.

Bhangra music

Originally, **bhangra** was the name for a kind of folk music from the Punjab, an area in northern India and Pakistan. In the 1980s, it also became the name for a popular style of dance music, which mixed traditional *bhangra* music with western **rhythms** and instruments, such as synthesizers and drum machines. *Bhangra* is a good example of fusion.

Traditional bhangra

Traditional Punjabi *bhangra* is a fast, energetic dance. Dancers are accompanied by folk singers and drummers playing the *dhol* drum. *Bhangra* is performed as part of the celebrations of the **Sikh** festival of *Vaisakhi*, which marks both the new year and the harvest festival. Some of the dance movements represent the actions of farmers at work in their fields. *Bhangra* is also performed at weddings and parties.

The new bhangra

The new style of *bhangra* was started in the UK by young Punjabis who were living there. It is now popular in Canada, the United States, and any country where Punjabi people live. It is also enjoyed by many non-Punjabi people. People go to clubs and dance to the beat of *bhangra* music. They often wear bright, sparkly clothes. There are *bhangra* singers, *bhangra* DJs, and *bhangra* dance groups. One very successful *bhangra* singer is called Jazzy B. He was born in the Punjab, grew up in Canada, and now lives in the UK. The development of *bhangra* perfectly illustrates how modern Asian music is made up of many different styles: old and new, Asian and western, and folk and pop.

Bhangra star Jazzy B performs at a Bollywood concert in London, 2006. His full name is Jaswinder Singh Bains.

New audiences

Nachda Sansaar are a group of *bhangra* musicians from the UK. They are very successful and they performed during the Eurovision Song Contest in 1998 and the Commonwealth Games in 2002. In 2006, they travelled to the Punjab and performed their style of *bhangra* to audiences there. *Bhangra* that had been created in the UK was being taken back to the place that had inspired it.

A world of music

	String Instruments	Brass Instruments	Wind Instruments
Africa	*oud* (**lute**), *rebec* (fiddle), *kora* (harp-lute), *ngoni* (harp), musical bow, one-string fiddle	*kakaki* or *wazi* (metal trumpets), horns made from animal horns	*naga*, *nay sodina* (flutes), *arghul*, *gaita* (single-reed instruments), *mizmar* (double-reed instrument)
Australia, Hawaii, and the Pacific	ukulele (modern), guitar (modern)		flutes, nose flutes, didgeridoo, conch shell horns
Eastern Asia	*erhu* (fiddle), *dan tranh*, *qin*, *koto*, *gayageum* (derived from *zithers*)	gongs, metallophones, xylophones	*shakuhachi* (flute), *khaen* (mouth organ), *sralai* (reed instrument)
Europe	violin, viola, cello, double bass, mandolin, guitar, lute, *zither*, hurdy gurdy (**folk** instruments)	trumpet, French horn, trombone, tuba	flute, recorder, oboe, clarinet, bassoon, bass clarinet, saxophone, accordion, bagpipes
Latin America and the Caribbean	*berimbau* (musical bow), *guitarrón* (bass guitar), *charango* (mandolin), *vilhuela* (high-pitched guitar)	trumpet, saxophone, trombone (salsa instruments)	*bandoneon* (button accordion)
Western Asia	**sitar**, *veena*, *oud*, *dombra*, *doutar*, *tar* (lutes), *rebab*, *kobyz* (fiddles), *sarod*, *santoor*, *sarangi*	trumpets	*bansuri*, *ney* (flutes), *pungi/been* (clarinets), *shehnai*, *sorna* (oboes), bagpipes

Percussion Instruments	Vocal Styles	Dance Styles
balafon (wooden xylophone), *mbira* (thumb piano), bells slit drums, friction drums, hourglass drums, and conventional drums	open throat singing, Arabic style singing: this is more nasal (in the nose) and includes many trills and ornaments	spiritual dancing, mass dances, team/formation dances, small group and solo dances, modern social dances
slit drums, rattles, drums, clapsticks, **gourds**, rolled mats	*oli* (sung by one person), *mele* (poetry), hula (type of *mele*), *himene* (choral music), Dreaming songs	hula (accompanies song), seated dances, *fa'ataupati* (clapping and slapping), haka (chant)
taiko (drums)	*p'ansori* (single singer), *chooimsae* (verbal encouragement), folk songs	Peking/Beijing opera, Korean folk dance
side drum, snare drum, tambourine, *timpani* (kettle drums), cymbals, castanets, bodhran, piano	solo ballad, work song, hymn, plainchant, opera, Music Hall, cabaret, choral, homophony (harmony, parts moving together), polyphony (independent vocals together)	jig, reel, sword dance, clog dance, *mazurka* (folk dances), flamenco, country dance, waltz, polka, ballet, *pavane, galliard* (16th century)
friction drum, steel drums, bongos (small drums), congas (large drums), *timbales* (shallow drums), maracas (shakers), *guiro* (scraper)	toasting	*zouk* (pop music), tango, lambada, samba, *bossa nova* (city music), rumba, mambo, *merengue* (salsa)
tabla drum, *dhol* drum, tambourine, *bartal* cymbals, bells, sticks, gongs	**bards**, **bhangra** (Punjabi), **qawwali** (Sufi music), throat singing, **ghazals** (love poems)	*bhangra, dabke* (traditional), Indian **classical**, whirling **dervishes**, belly dancing

Glossary

Arab person who speaks Arabic

bard type of poet who recites poems
from memory

bhangra type of folk music from the Punjab area
of northern India and Pakistan. Also a style of
dance music that started in the UK in the 1980s.

Bollywood name given to the Indian film
industry in the city of Mumbai (Mumbai used
to be called Bombay)

classical music that is composed and
written down

dervish religious man who follows the religion
of Sufism and performs spinning dances

folk music that is handed down in communities
over many years

fusion joining together two or more things,
such as two musical styles

ghazal love poem set to music

gourd hard, dried skin of a fruit or vegetable,
used to make parts of some instruments

Hinduism ancient religion whose followers, called
Hindus, believe in many gods and goddesses

improvise make up the words or notes to
a song or piece of music

independent free from control

Islam religion whose followers, called Muslims,
believe in one god called Allah

jazz type of American popular music that has
strong rhythms and is based on improvisation
(making music up on the spot)

lute plucked, stringed instrument with long neck
and pear-shaped body with flat front

maqaam pattern of notes in Middle Eastern music

nomad person who travels around instead of
living in one place

percussion instrument instrument that makes
a sound when hit or shaken

qawwali type of Sufi music and singing from
Pakistan and north India

raga pattern of notes in Indian classical music.
Also a piece of improvised music.

rhythm beat behind a piece of music

sari Indian woman's dress made of a large piece
of material draped carefully around the body

scale set of notes that goes up and down

shrine holy place, usually marked with a building

Sikhism religion that began in the 1400s,
in the Punjab area of South Asia (Northern
India and Pakistan)

sitar stringed instrument played in North India

stringed instrument instrument played by
plucking, bowing, or hitting strings

tabla Indian drum

tala rhythm pattern in Indian classical music

throat singing style of singing where the
singer moves their mouth, tongue, and teeth in
a particular way so that two notes are sung at
the same time

wind instrument instrument that is blown.
The sound is either produced by vibrating reeds,
or by air vibrating over a hole.

Further information

Books

O'Brien, Eileen. *Introduction to Music* (Usborne, 2003)

Wade-Matthews, Max. *Illustrated Encyclopedia of Musical Instruments* (Lorenz Books, 2004)

Websites

Middle Eastern musicians
www.arabiannights.ca/music.html

Journey across central Asia
www.bbc.co.uk/nomad/

Indian music and culture
www.bbc.co.uk/radio3/world/onyourstreet/thestreet/india/

Indian classical dances
www.kanakasabha.com

Sevara Nazarkhan
www.sevaranazarkhan.calabashmusic.com/

Places to visit

Each of these museums has collections of musical instruments from around the world:

Horniman Museum
100 London Road
Forest Hill
London, SE23 3PQ,
U.K
http://www.horniman.ac.uk/

Pitt Rivers Museum
Oxford University Museum of Natural History
Parks Road
Oxford, OX1 3PW
U.K
http://www.prm.ox.ac.uk/

Australian Museum
6 College Street
Sydney, NSW 2010
Australia
http://www.amonline.net.au/

Index